THE ART OF TEAMWORK

Maximise your results by working together

Written by Caroline Cailteux

Translated by Emma Lunt

Coaching 50MINUTES.com

THE ART OF TEAMWORK

- **Issue:** what position should I occupy in a team in order to collaborate effectively with all members?
- **Uses:** good teamwork allows each person's contributions and collaborations to be optimised, which influences the organisation's productivity.
- **Professional context:** human resource management, teamwork, project management.
- **FAQs:**
  - What are the characteristics of a professional team?
  - What elements are favourable to the effective functioning of a team?
  - Does the interdependence of tasks influence efficiency?
  - Is there a model for evaluating team performance?
  - Can a team's performance be evaluated based on its results?
  - Are the highest-performing team members the ones that get the best results?
  - Is performance linked only to skills?
  - Does the team have an impact on my personal identity?

The group in which we work influences our individual performance at work. As each team develops their own dynamic, the individuals within it develop connections every day that form standards for expected behaviour and routines that should be respected. Beyond individual and collective skills, which are used to work towards a common goal, being effective requires identifying these operating codes and taking on different roles. This framework of collective standards puts a fairly strong pressure on your actions, by either cultivating or failing to cultivate your interpersonal comfort within the team. Although they are very present and influence the involvement of group members, these standards are unfortunately not always as explicit as we would like. Consequently, upon contact with a team, your challenge will be positioning yourself appropriately within it in order to fit into its particular dynamic.

Groups are like ships that cross the oceans. It is a matter of reaching the other shore by taking the good waves, by crossing storms and by making the most of the periods of calm following these two actions. Neglecting the characteristics and dynamics of the group could cancel out the efforts of your involvement at work. For this reason, we are suggesting that you spend 50 minutes discovering solutions that, we hope, will help you to define which position best suits you in order to experience a smooth crossing.

While researchers have been focused for a long time on what happens within groups in order to better understand the impact on individuals, today organisations (particularly for-profit organisations) are asking themselves questions about the performance of a group and the consequences of its actions on the company's overall productivity. In fact, if we form teams, it is, among other reasons, because we are not experts in all subjects and we need other peoples' skills in order to successfully complete a project. Teams are a way of mobilising a wide range of resources (similar or complementary) so as to achieve a common goal.

Beyond teams themselves, the context in which a team evolves and the environmental factors that influence its efficiency are also emphasised through advice and questions and answers. While the performance of teams plays a considerable role in the productivity of an organisation, the organisation's environment in turn affects team results.

EFFECTIVE TEAMWORK: THE BASICS

In order to fuel reflection on your effectiveness within a work team, we suggest that you reflect on your position according to these three approaches:

- **The individual approach:** what are your personal comfort and effort zones in your personal functioning?
- **The collective approach:** what is your position within the team and your role in terms of functioning and relationships?
- **The environmental approach:** what are the logics which justify the actions underlying the dominant characteristics in your work environment?

POSITIONING YOURSELF INDIVIDUALLY

Some of your colleagues are kind to you and you find it easy to collaborate with them, whereas you feel incapable of working with others. The following section will provide you with some key ideas that should help you to understand why some working relationships function and others do not.

This approach was inspired by the work of Carl Gustav Jung (1921) on psychological types. The main underlying idea of this approach is to identify your preferences regarding situations, objects, people, etc.

INTRODUCTORY EXERCISE

1. Write your name and address with the hand that you usually write with.
2. Write the same thing, but this time with your other hand.

What did you find easy and difficult? The first exercise probably seemed much more simple to you than the second. By using your dominant hand, you found yourself in your comfort zone. Were you less agile when using the other hand? Did it take you longer to write? Did you have to concentrate more? Is the result of identical quality? By using the other hand, in a non-spontaneous situation, you have shown yourself to be capable of doing the exercise, but in your effort zone.

Our spontaneous preferences regarding people or situations require us to use less energy than when we are faced with the opposite case. Our energy therefore takes orientation direction, positioning itself on an axis that stretches between two opposing poles, with a natural preference for one side of the axis rather than the other:

Psychological types

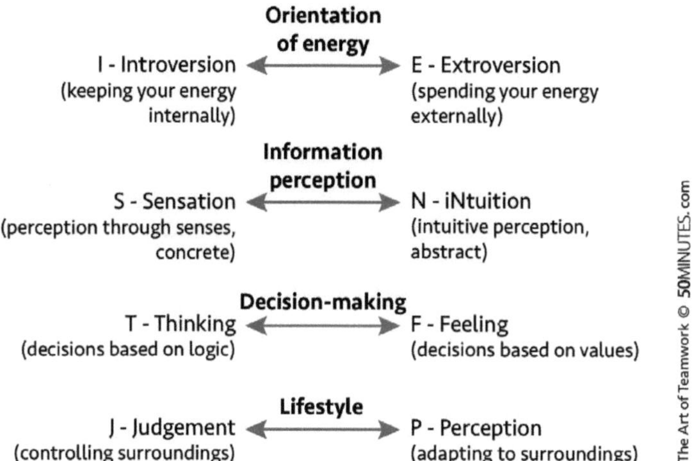

The combination of positions on these four axes enables us to map out 16 profiles that characterise different ways of functioning in our private and professional lives. Do not hesitate to take the MBTI (Myers-Briggs Type Indicator) test to determine your preferred way of functioning. By understanding the basics of your profile, you will better understand why you love handling files with Marcus, why you hate Rita's lack of organisation, or why you feel irritated by your superior's digressions during meetings.

Extraversion (E) versus Introversion (I)

When Marion enters the office, she always seems well. She is naturally sociable, so she goes around the team, exchanging a few words, and even some laughter with some people. When she arrives, everybody knows it. Marion's energy is probably positioned towards the extraversion pole (E). Although he finds her nice, Igor is exhausted just watching Marion's morning routine. He is naturally reserved and rational, and arrives early in the morning, allowing him to gently ease into the working day and to have a little privacy. When Marion sits down opposite him, he is already focused and feels a little disturbed by her chatting. Igor undoubtedly has an energy oriented towards introversion (I).

Sensation (S) versus iNtuition (N)

Suddenly, Marion calls out to Igor: "Have you seen the new poster by the entrance?". "The one with the beach and three palm trees, with the writing in italics?" Igor asks. He refers to concrete information in a structured and realistic manner (S). Marion replies "Erm, I mean the one that makes you dream, that reminds you of holidays and gives you a feeling of escape, some fresh air before you go into the office." Based on her intuition (N), Marion lets herself be carried away by her imagination.

Thinking (T) versus Feeling (F)

Their supervisor is pondering whether or not to renew a project. He invites Marion and Igor to give their opinions on the issue. Marion exclaims: "I think that we have to keep the project. It allows us to convey and reinforce the organisation's social image. Regular customers will be really disappointed if we do not organise the event. It is also one of the few opportunities that enables us to spend time together as a team. What do you think Igor?" Igor takes the document that he prepared that morning, identifying the strengths and weaknesses of the project and decides: "Objectively, if I look at my analyses and at the budget, I would opt not to relaunch the event." These exchanges lead us to believe that Marion's decisions come from her feelings and values (F), while Igor makes his decisions based on what seems logical to him (T).

Judgement (J) versus Perception (P)

While Igor likes to have some control over events (J), Marion's lifestyle invites her to seize opportunities (P). "Come on Igor," Marion insists, "it's a chance to meet people and to make discoveries." Igor gives in. "I'll agree on one condition. We rethink the organisation of the events and have everything ready on time. This is not a case of you arriving late and us finding ourselves out in the rain because you have forgotten to rent a tent!" Marion replies: "I think you're being a bit harsh. We took shelter under the trees and everything was fine!"

Finding your role in the work

The composition of your team influences its effectiveness. According to studies by some researchers, the challenge lies not so much in forming a heterogeneous team (its heterogeneous nature will not affect its effectiveness), but in forming a team that is appropriate for the task it is responsible for.

In order for team members to be able to coordinate their actions in a coherent manner, it is important that each person has clear ideas on the priority tasks that they will have to carry out. It is not rare to see people get into a conflict because they step on other people's toes, or blame each other for a task not being done.

EXAMPLE

Lucie systematically goes to the desk to welcome new clients, while Marco is the one who is supposed to take care of greeting clients. Lucie thinks she is helping her colleague and does not realise that her initiatives are frustrating for Marco, who feels that it is impossible for him to accomplish his task. While they argue about the desk, nobody hands out the post, which may contain important or urgent demands from clients that should be dealt with.

The relevant distribution of responsibilities is necessary for a team to function well. Again, we all have our 'comfort zones' (the things that we can do easily and spontaneously) and our 'effort zones' (the things that we do that require effort, learning or more concentration). Correctly identifying the areas of work and skill profiles of team members enables roles to be distributed in relation to functions, which leads to tasks being done more efficiently.

The theoretical model "mapping of the coexistence of functions and skills"[1] (Cailteux, 2013) suggests describing the role played by each person, within the framework of the function attributed to them, by dividing the activities done into three categories:

- **predominantly pragmatic or managerial activities,** which use the reproduction of gestures and procedures, in relatively similar situations, centred around objects and concrete realisations;
- **predominantly cognitive activities,** which use cerebral processes, reflection, extrapolation in unknown or new areas, centred around abstract elements and the search for solutions;
- **predominantly interpersonal activities,** which use the method of understanding interactions with people and reacting to the environment, centred around emotional aspects, values and implementing methods.

While every job is likely to include these three dimensions and we are potentially capable of executing our skills in the

---

1. This quotation has been translated by 50Minutes.com.

three domains, every function needs to establish its priorities, favouring some activities over others. By determining these priorities, profiles can fit together, playing on universal or complementary aspects. The interaction of these three dimensions gives rise to eight 'functional roles', which require the activation of a combination of skills that are directly linked to the execution of the prescribed tasks. Each job can be carried out by emphasising one or more domains.

Functional role	Will focus primarily on...	Examples
Operator	predominantly pragmatic activities, centred around material realisation.	Cleaners, labourers, administrative support...
Specialist	predominantly cognitive activities, focused on ideas and solutions.	Experts on a sector's specific files, researchers, chemists, analysts...
Accompanier	predominantly relational activities, confronting emotional reactions.	Social assistants, employment advisers...
Intermediary	the combination of pragmatic and relational activities, putting their money where their mouth is to satisfy a customer.	Over-the-counter sellers, reception staff, counter staff...
Transmitter	the combination of relational and cognitive activities, transforming data and information to improve transmission to the target audience.	Those in charge of communication, trainers, teachers...

Functional role	Will focus primarily on...	Examples
Administrator	the combination of cognitive and managerial activities, adapting actions by analysing new situations to ensure the continuity of processes.	Administrator of administrative files, administrator of technical processes...
Co-ordinator	the combination of reflection and action, by taking care of relational aspects, without exerting power over the target group, but by mobilising them.	Coordinator of project X...
Manager	the combination of reflection and action, by taking care of relational aspects, exerting leadership and authority over the target group attributed and legitimised by the organisation.	Manager of commercial teams...

No job is definitively linked to one of these categories; what is important is the role attributed within the function. For example, a plumber can play the role of an operator who repairs leaks according to instructions, an administrator who analyses the issue before repairing the leak, a transmitter who comes up with plumbing techniques or a manager who gives orders to the team and explains how to fix the leaks.

Within a team, each person plays two types of roles (Belbin, 2006):

- **A functional role,** which the organisation wants to see

you develop within your duties. It describes the way in which you are supposed to do your tasks compared to others (in an identical or complementary manner).
- **A team role,** which concerns the way in which you are going to organise your relations with other people.

Indeed, if two people prove to be capable of organising events, handling files or managing an IT network, it may be the case that one of them is more or less effective when put to work with a team. No two people are the same and some team compositions suit us better according to the role we will have the chance to play on an interpersonal level. We are not simple robots. To be effective in a team, we cannot be satisfied with 'functioning'. Beyond our functional role, it is important to identify our comfort zones and effort zones within our relationships with our colleagues, or our 'team role'.

Positioning yourself within the team

Meredith Belbin describes nine 'team roles', characterising our behaviour regarding group members and the way in which we personally contribute. According to her approach, three roles correspond to us, and some roles require more energy than others. Taking these elements into account enables us to understand why we can be competent without managing to demonstrate it within certain teams, while we excel when working with other colleagues.

It should be noted that while they share some of the same terms, the roles described below are different to the functional roles described above. The following information does not concern the function attributed by the organisation, but rather the attitude that the person will develop upon contact with their team! Here are the nine roles as defined by the author, based on the behaviour that is likely to contribute to a team's success, and their weaknesses:

Identifying the roles at play in a team will enable responsibilities to be distributed evenly, taking into account the affinities of different people (even though it is of course impossible to apply this approach 100% in practice).

Belbin's team roles	Strengths	Things to pay attention to…
Monitor evaluator	Strategic, considers opinions analytically.	Can be perceived as being critical and lacking dynamism.
Specialist	Independent and determined, focuses on objectives. Resourceful in terms of knowledge and techniques.	Neglects wider reading in order to focus on technical dimensions. They are competent, but in a narrow domain.
Implementer	Methodical and disciplined, transforms ideas into concrete actions.	Lacks flexibility and is resistant to new ideas.
Shaper	Dynamic and a go-getter, overcomes challenges and is effective under pressure. Encourages others into action.	Can be offensive without meaning to be.
Complete finisher	Conscientiously looks for mistakes and ensures that deadlines are respected and the work is perfect.	Too worried about details, can worry excessively.

Belbin's team roles	Strengths	Things to pay attention to...
Co-ordinator	Confident and diplomatic, encourages decisions and ensures optimisation of the use of team member's qualities.	Can be perceived as manipulative.
Plant	Creative and non-conformist, resolves problems by generating ideas.	Neglects details and worries little about communication.
Resource innovator	Enthusiastic, studies and exploits opportunities. Develops a network of contacts.	Sometimes lacks realism and their enthusiasm subsides.
Teamworker	Sociable, sensitive and obliging, takes care of the needs of others and avoids tensions within the team.	Influenceable, can prove to be indecisive and feel uncomfortable when faced with conflict.

POSITIONING YOURSELF ACCORDING TO THE GROUP DYNAMIC

Sustained or reduced pace of work?

You will not be surprised to hear that a group's standards have a certain influence on the efforts of its members.

- Does your team's standard lead to a high level of demand? Do your colleagues expect that you will put intensive effort into your work? Do the members of your team tend to stay after their official hours in order to finalise their projects?

- Or is it the opposite? Do your colleagues tend to tell you: "Hey, slow the pace, the person before you didn't use to do so much. Relax!"?

Many studies have shown that if the group's standard places the bar higher in terms of the amount of effort put into work, group members will tend to adhere to it, even if this means making sacrifices such as staying at the office after hours, for example to complete a project. On the contrary, if the standard is to put moderate effort into work, it has been observed that group members will also adhere to this. Group members tend to encourage new recruits to take it easy if they are doing too much compared to others. This can already help you to better understand many things regarding work dynamics within a group.

- Do you tend to follow the increased or reduced pace of the team and to position yourself within the norm to avoid tension? Does this suit you?
- Do you tend to break with the norm, returning home early when the others are working flat out (or doing too much in your opinion) or are you the rare bird that leaves the office in the dark when the caretaker is about to close the doors, when your colleagues have long since returned home? Does this suit you?

The working environment and standards of the team will have a considerable impact on motivation and involvement at work. Professional performance is not always just a question of competence. If you love your job and you feel competent, but you feel uncomfortable every day within your team, it may be that its norms, including its pace of work, do not suit you.

Fair or unfair? Conventional or not?

If we size one another up based on the efforts invested in work, teamwork also raises the question of the justification for the work carried out.

- Some teams interact a lot, allowing each person to really understand what the other is doing and to develop a form of empathy.

    I helped Pierre to finish off the budget last year, I understand how stressful it is!
    In our team, everybody pitches in. When we organise meetings, we take care of the coffee just as we do the writing of the minutes, and we make sure to take it in turns.

- In other teams, interactions are less frequent. Although group members work in the same place, interactions are rare, with each person working on their own area and doing their own job, which can quickly lead to tensions:

    What is he still doing? He's never sat at his desk, he spends all his time in the restaurant with clients!
    Pfft, she never looks away from her computer, it's easy, all she has to do is encode figures, while I have to negotiate with clients to make profits.

Although we are not formally obliged to do so, teamwork leads us to regularly seek justifications for our way of working.

Carole has been part of the organisation since it began. She has always proven to be loyal to the boss, who gave her a chance when she had just got divorced. In order to thank him, she is disciplined, is never absent, always arrives on time and handles as many files as possible each day. When she returns home, she feels calm and has a strong sense of having accomplished her task efficiently. This is her way of showing her loyalty to her employer.

Since the sales team's arrival, however, Carole feels a lot of tension. She struggles to understand how her superior tolerates this 'gang of youths' who spend their time on the phone, justifying their late arrival to the office by the fact that their work depends on results and not on the number of hours worked. Although she does not like his working methods nor the fact that he seems like a baby in a suit, she tries to tolerate Mark because her boss is happy with his work. The revenue has in fact increased considerably since his arrival thanks to his talents as a negotiator. Carole is magnanimous, but waits to see how it goes.

Why has Carole felt uncomfortable since the young salespeople arrived? With a doubt, it is because the group dynamic as well as its justifications for work have changed since the organisation began. While Carole justifies her behaviour through respect for traditions, loyalty towards her superior and the application of effective methods, in terms of daily productivity, Mark and the salespeople focus on the organisation's image and think only of profit. Carole questions herself. Is her boss disappointed in her? Has he forgotten her years of loyal service? What could she do? She invites Mark to lunch, swallows her pride and asks him for advice. He encourages her to adopt a more dynamic attitude, to smile more and to show herself to be concerned about the needs of her customers. He helps her to arrange her working space to improve the atmosphere and the quality of the customer's reception. On returning from a business trip, the boss notices Carole's new behaviour, is surprised by the changes and is satisfied by this new contribution to the organisation's brand image. For the first time in a long time, he greets Carole warmly and congratulates her.

What happened? While at first the priority values centred around loyalty and productivity, nowadays, it seems that the emphasis is on the brand image and profit. For all these years, Carole had perhaps not understood how much of a priority customer opinion and the organisation's reputation were for her employer. This priority has been accentuated by the arrival of the salespeople and Carole focuses on adapting, with the help of Mark. By working on her customer focus, Carole moves towards the team priorities which relate to the organisation's reputation.

Boltanski and Thévenot are the authors of *On Justification: Economies of Worth* (2006), which aims to explore the types of justification people use to legitimise their actions.

According to this approach, it is the situation that is at the heart of the analysis. This means identifying the way in which people build their argument and logic to determine what is fair and what is not. It is not surprising to learn that brand image and people's opinions are considered important in the style or marketing sectors, since creativity will be a priority for a cultural centre. Consequently, we call on a combination of "economies of worth" to explain why we act in one way and not another, according to the justifications that seem to be a priority for us.

In case of conflict, people call on higher principles, which they share, to define what is right to do – a bit like a common denominator that makes everybody see eye to eye. The authors talk about "principles" rather than values, considering that the former are more linked to situations, while values are linked to people. The economies of worth are "like logics of justification based on an idea of the common good"[2] (Jacquemain, 2001: 13). In this approach, agreement between parties and acceptable arguments will vary from one economy of worth to another. When people agree on what was the right thing to do, the dispute ends.

While this approach is usually positioned on the level of analysis of institutions and policies, it is also interesting to observe the functioning of a team from the point of view of economies of worth (explained below). If you are having difficulty justifying your actions to your team, and if your arguments seem unacceptable when you are in conflict

---

2. This quotation has been translated by 50Minutes.com.

with your colleagues, it may be interesting to check if your logics of argumentation correspond to those preferred by the team.

Economies of worth

Economy of worth	Main common principle that can produce compliance and agreement among people
Civic	Representativeness – collectiveness: things that are the result of a vote are fair
Market	Commitment – loyalty – tradition: things that enable tradition to continue are fair
Inspired	Effectiveness – implementation: things that effectively mobilise the means necessary are fair
Fame	Renown – notoriety: things that make them famous or popular are fair
Industrial	Creativity – inspiration – authenticity: things that are loyal to their inspiration are fair
Domestic	Interest – the desire to possess – profit: things that enable them to possess more are fair

TOP TIPS

PAY ATTENTION TO TEAM COHESION

Cohesion is the invisible glue of your team, an essential element for its balance and thus its effectiveness. This is the thing that holds everything together through different types of attraction between individuals. Research into the relationships between different people from the same group show that in order to strengthen and develop the cohesion of a team – and therefore its effectiveness – it is particularly necessary to take care of the following aspects:

- cultivating a positive team image;
- aiming to achieve common objectives;
- taking care to reinforce the feeling of security;
- highlighting team actions;
- being aware of the added value of collective actions compared to individual actions;
- nurturing affinities within the team;
- avoiding the isolation of a team member.

BE AWARE OF THE TOXICITY OF CERTAIN BEHAVIOURS

While teamwork enables us to improve our performance in some ways, this professional cohabitation can sometimes prove difficult to manage. As we previously saw, some collaborations use more of our energy, as some profiles do not suit us at all and we perceive the attitudes of these people as 'toxic'.

If you reveal your opinions to a colleague, they may be surprised by them. In fact, what is unpleasant for one person may not be for the other.

FOUR LEVELS OF REACTION IN THE PRESENCE OF A TOXIC PERSON

- Emotional: bad mood, feeling of worthlessness, feeling of being drained of all energy, feeling of inferiority, irritability, feeling of not existing, etc.
- Behavioural: desire to distance yourself, avoidance, submissive or aggressive attitude, etc.
- Physical: headaches, nausea, difficulty breathing, dry throat, nervous tics, etc.
- Communication: feeling of having to walk on eggshells, changing tone of voice, need to shout, defensive nonverbal behaviour, feeling of double meaning during interactions, etc.

The following table takes up some of the ideas put forward by Lillian Glass (1995) for dealing with toxic profiles. Make sure you do not lose sight of the fact that we can all potentially be somebody else's toxic agent. Relationships can be constructive when points of tension are identified and both parties agree to take a step forwards.

Toxic Profile	Advice
The Cut-You-Downer Often demonstrates a feeling of insecurity.	Ask them what bothers them about your behaviour and what drives them to make the comments they do. The aim of these questions is to identify what bothers the person to defuse the tension.
The Chatterbox Needs to be accepted and loved to feel important.	Speak to the person to let them know that you are worried about them. Calmly explain to them (one on one) that they are speaking too much, often saying nothing, and at inappropriate times. If possible, come up with a sign to signal to them in the future when you have reached your limit with them.
The Gossip Feels insecure and lacks self-esteem.	Let them know that you have not fallen for their little game. Show them that their behaviour is unacceptable and cut them off when they start to spread rumours to you about others. Or cut contact.
The Opportunistic User Selfish, disloyal and manipulative.	Confront them and directly explain that you feel exploited and offended by their behaviour. Or cut contact.

INTERPRET SITUATIONS WITH PROFESSIONALISM

If you want to position yourself and earn the respect of your peers, it can prove useful to not be satisfied with being the 'average colleague' and showing yourself as professional. According to Guy Le Boterf (2010), it is not enough to know how to execute the tasks set for others to benefit from your skills. A professional also proves capable of facing up to unexpected situations.

Beyond the instructions that are given to your team, in order to show professionalism, you should correctly interpret situations that you are faced with. The challenge will be working out what behaviour is expected, according to the norms relevant to the group.

As Le Boterf indicates, the emphasis is not so much on 'know-how' but rather on 'know-what' in order to make good decisions.

The situations we find ourselves in are overflowing with information; it is well worth identifying that which is relevant, as otherwise you risk investing energy in useless, or even inappropriate, behaviour. You will certainly already have heard a close friend confide in you: "I don't understand, I'm capable, I do everything I can, I meet deadlines and they are still not happy." You will certainly be giving good advice if you invite your friend to analyse the situation and to check if the results that they produce correspond with the implicit expectations of their team.

And that is the trick. In order to be professional and high-performing in a team, it is not enough to refer to the explicit: you must also try to deduce the hazy aspects of the situation and use your sense of observation. Whatever you might think about a situation, "knowing how to act is also sometimes about knowing to choose not to intervene"[3] (Le

---

3. This quotation has been translated by 50Minutes.com.

Boterf, 2010: 26). Consequently, do not trust appearances, leave nothing to chance and put out your feelers!

FAQS

WHAT ARE THE CHARACTERISTICS OF A PROFESSIONAL TEAM?

According to Alderfer (1977) and Hackman (1987) (cited in Guzzo, 1996: 7-8), working groups share the following characteristics:

- they are social entities that are part of a larger system (for example, an organisation's legal department);
- they carry out one or more shared tasks for the organisation (the management of legal files);
- their performance in their tasks impacts the organisation (the poor management of a legal file could lead to the loss of a trial for the company);
- they are made up of individuals who have relatively interdependent roles;
- it is perceptible that people belong to the group as much from inside as outside the group (members of the legal department and members of other departments within the organisation perceive the identity and existence of the team).

WHAT ELEMENTS ARE FAVOURABLE TO THE EFFECTIVE FUNCTIONING OF A TEAM?

In order for a team to have a reason to exist, all its members must contribute to the production of goods and/or services that are expected of them. A team's effectiveness depends on the convergence, coordination and persistence of the individual efforts of its members. Various studies have enabled us to identify the factors that are likely to positively influence a team's productivity;

- interpersonal support, which promotes the longevity of the team;
- resource management, which essentially concerns the execution of tasks;
- support for innovation, promoting continuous improvement.

Each individual cannot fulfil all these tasks alone, and so the identification of different people's roles within the team will enable a clearer representation of the contributions that you and your colleagues can provide to the production.

DOES THE INTERDEPENDENCE OF TASKS INFLUENCE EFFICIENCY?

Yes. According to Catherine Guertin, André Savoie and Claude Larivière (2003), the interdependence of the members of a team (in terms of tasks, objectives and feedback) influences its effectiveness. The more you rely on your colleagues in the execution of your role, the more your goals will be shared. The more the results of your actions depend on collective contribution, the more your team should be evaluated as efficient by you and your colleagues. The results of their research indicate that objectives defined as a group have a definitive effect on its effectiveness. In order to work well with your colleagues, it is therefore important that you have shared goals.

<u>**ARE YOU FAMILIAR WITH THE BIRG EFFECT?**</u>

You will certainly have had the chance to experience, during your private or professional life, the extent to which people tend to think failures and problems are 'yours'. They tell you "**You** should have done that. Why didn't **you** do that?" On the contrary, when it is about success, team members are quick to tell you: "It's great, **we** have succeeded!"

This infuriating phenomenon of appropriation of others' victories and success, without having actually contributed, is explained by the BIRG (Basking In Reflected Glory) effect. This psychological strategy is used by individuals to reinforce their personal esteem towards others, and is related to the fact that that our personal identities are connected to our social identities, meaning those that stem from our feeling of belonging to different social groups.

IS THERE A MODEL TO EVALUATE TEAM PERFORMANCE?

Yes. The *"input-process-output of work team performance"* model by Joseph E. McGrath (1964) continues to be one of the most influential performance models. It is frequently used to study team performance.

- The *inputs*, or resources invested in a project, consist of the knowledge, skills and experience of team members,

as well as the means at their disposal.
* The *outputs,* or results achieved, are the team performance, the satisfaction of its members and its viability.

Resources become results following different transforma-
tion processes, and McGrath's model invites us to focus on
these processes rather than on resources or results when
analysing team effectiveness.

CAN A TEAM'S PERFORMANCE BE EVA-LUATED BASED ON ITS RESULTS?

Team performance cannot be evaluated based on results
alone. According to many organisational psychologists,
performance is not the result of an action, but the action
itself. Why not take results as performance indicators? Put
simply, it is because the achievement of results is not totally
controlled by the person or the team. Many factors can hin-
der the realisation of actions: lack of means, poor working
conditions, lack of collaboration between different parties,
etc. If you wish to evaluate the effectiveness of your team,
it will be necessary for you to look closely at the following
mechanisms:

* coordination
* communication
* cohesion
* decision-making
* conflict management
* interpersonal relations
* feedback on the team's productivity.

ARE THE HIGHEST-PERFORMING TEAM MEMBERS THE ONES THAT GET THE BEST RESULTS?

Not necessarily. As we explained above, performance does not depend so much on the results of the actions undertaken as on behaviour at the time of the action. Performance is what we physically do. Results are the product of our performance and are not only connected to our actions. The achievement of individual and collective objectives also depends on factors that are outside our control, such as the contribution of other teams in the process, the availability of resources, managerial impact, interest in the process, etc.

Perhaps you admire Emily, who always finishes her files on time, or Victor, who lands big contracts. You may also think that Julia is not very involved in her work, because her organisational change project was unsuccessful, whereas she has the chance to participate in innovative activities and the opportunity to collaborate with important people.

We are easily tempted to believe that the high-performing people are those that obtain visible results. But this belief is only correct if the result is totally under that person's control, and is identifiable and demonstrable. Perhaps Emily does not feel the need to tell you that Patrick helped her encode the data to save time, and that Victor has a network of connections who are

Before judging a colleague's performance (or lack thereof),
it is good to analyse the context and to speak to them in
order to see the situation objectively.

IS PERFORMANCE LINKED ONLY TO SKILLS?

No. A number of studies have shown that behaviour like
helping, sharing or collaborating contribute to the feeling of
wellbeing and to the integration of people at work. Scientists
who study organisations have focused their attention on
these 'prosocial behaviours' which also influence organisational performance. This concerns the selfless behaviour of
some people which benefits others (such as collaborating)
or the organisation (such as speaking positively about the
organisation outside the office).

'Organisational citizenship' behaviour is a type of prosocial
behaviour that is not considered in the formal performance
evaluation system, but that contributes to the effective
functioning of organisations. This behaviour is shown, for
example, through politeness (warning people if you will be
absent), selflessness (helping a colleague who has too much
work), team spirit (accepting exceptional constraints without complaining), civic virtues (being present at funerals,

parties), etc.

In actual fact, it refers to so-called 'discretionary' behaviour, meaning that people act in this way voluntarily. The factors that contribute to the appearance of such behaviours are the support of a superior, the interdependence of tasks between team members, job satisfaction, organisational involvement and procedural justice (the workers see procedures as being fairly carried out).

DOES THE TEAM HAVE AN IMPACT ON MY PERSONAL IDENTITY?

To an extent. Tajfel and Turner (1979), specialists in social identity theory, state that individuals seek to positively differentiate their group by comparing it to others, with the goal of forging a positive social identity. When we are part of a team, we develop a social identity, a feeling of belonging to this group, which plays a role in our individual identity.

"WE ARE THE BEST" OR PRO-INGROUP BIAS

Many researchers have shown that we tend to think the group we belong to and our products are superior to other groups and what they produce. Once again, in this type of situation, our social identity and our need to positively distinguish ourselves leads us to choose to positively evaluate our own team. Thinking that our group is better than others helps us to feel better and to thrive within it.

OVER TO YOU

Positioning yourself within the work

What is my functional role?
- Operator
- Intermediary
- Accompanier
- Transmitter
- Specialist
- Administrator
- Co-ordinator
- Manager

Positioning yourself within the team

What is my role in the team?
- Monitor evaluator
- Specialist
- Implementer
- Shaper
- Complete finisher
- Co-ordinator
- Plant
- Resource innovator
- Teamworker

Positioning yourself individually

Introversion – Extroversion
Sensation – Intuition
Thinking – Feeling
Judgement – Perception

Pay attention to and increase effectiveness through:

- coordination
- communication
- cohesion
- decision-making
- conflict management
- social relationships
- feedback on the team's productivity

+ Professionalism
+ Pro-social behaviour
- Toxic behaviour

Positioning yourself in the situation

Increased or reduced pace?

Modes of justification of actions?
- Civic economy of worth
- Domestic economy of worth
- Industrial economy of worth
- Fame economy of worth
- Inspired economy of worth
- Market economy of worth

FURTHER READING

BIBLIOGRAPHY

- Belbin, M. (2006) *Les rôles en équipe.* Paris: Éditions d'Organisation.
- Borden, R.J., Cialdini, R.B. et al. (1976) Basking in Reflected Glory: Three (Football) Fields Studies. *Journal of Personality and Social Psychology.* 34(3), pp. 366-375.
- Brief, A.P. and Motowidlo, S.J. (1986) Prosocial Organizational Behaviors. *The Academy of Management Review.* 11(4), pp. 710-725.
- Cailloux, G. et Cauvin, P. (1994) *Deviens qui tu es. Guide pratique.* Gap (France): Le souffle d'Or.
- Cailteux, C. (2013) *La gestion des compétences. Du modèle à la pratique.* Bruges (Belgium): Vanden Broele.
- Delobbe, N., Karnas, G. and Vandenberghe, C. (2003) *Dimensions individuelles et sociales de l'investissement professional.* Vol. 2. Louvain-La-Neuve: Presses universitaires UCL.
- Doise, W. and Deschamps, J-C. (1969) *Expériences entre groupes.* Paris: Mouton éditeur. pp. 69-86.
- Glass, L. (1995) *Toxic People: 10 Ways of Dealing With People Who Make Your Life Miserable.* Beverley Hills: Your Total Image Publishing.
- Gosling, P. et al. (1996) *Psychologie sociale. L'individu et le groupe.* Levallois-Perret: Bréal.
- Jacquemain, M. (2001) Les cités et les mondes: le modèle de la justification chez Boltanski et Thevenot. *Département de sciences sociales de l'université de Liège.* [Online]. [Accessed 9 June 2015]. Available from:

<http://orbi.ulg.ac.be/bitstream/2268/90443/1/Les%20 cit%C3%A9s%20et%20les%20mondes%20de%20 Luc%20Boltanski.pdf>

- Jung, C-G. (1983) *Types psychologiques*. 5th edition. Geneva: Librairie de l'université George et Cie.
- Le Boterf, G. (2010) *Professionnaliser. Construire des parcours personnalisés de professionnalisation*. Paris: Éditions d'Organisation.
- Murphy, K.R. (1996) *Individual Differences and Behavior in Organizations*. San Francisco: Jossey-Bass. pp. 258-299.
- Solar, C. (2001) *Équipe de travail efficace. Savoirs et temps d'action*. Quebec: Les Éditions Logiques.
- West, M.A. (1996) *Handbook of Group Psychology*. Chichester: John Wiley & Sons.
- Worchel, S. and Austin, W.G. (1979) *Psychology of Intergroup Relations*. Chicago: Nelson-Hall. pp. 7-24.
- Yeatts, D.E. and Hyten, C. (1998) *High-Performing Self-Managed Work Teams. A Comparison of Theory to Practice*. Thousand Oaks: Sage Publications.

ADDITIONAL SOURCES

- McChrystal, G. with Collins, T., Silverman, D. and Fussell, C. (2015) *Team of Teams: New Rules of Engagement for a Complex World*. New York: Penguin.
- West, M.A. (2012) *Effective Teamwork: Practical Lessons from Organizational Research (Psychology of Work and Organizations)*. London: Blackwell Publishing.

IMPROVE YOUR GENERAL KNOWLEDGE

IN A BLINK OF AN EYE !

www.50minutes.com